ITALIAN

Clare Jakens

Illustrated by Joseph McEwan

Language consultants: Paola Boutall,

Patrizia Di Bello, Loredana Pasini

Ciao

Parli italiano?

Sí

Designed by Graham Round

Edited by Roby

Contents

First published in 1982 by
Usborne Publishing Ltd.
20 Garrick Street, London WC2E 9BJ,
England

Manufactured in Great Britain
by Blantyre Printing & Binding Ltd.,
London & Glasgow

How to use this Book

This book will help you make yourself understood in most everyday situations when you are on holiday or travelling in Italy. The phrases have been kept as simple as possible, and include some of the possible answers to the questions you may want to ask. There are also translations of many of the signs you will see.

The book is divided into sections, each covering a situation you are likely to find yourself in. Use the contents list at the front or the index at the back to help you find the pages you need. You will find it easier if you look up the section you are going to need in advance, so you can practise saying the phrases.

For most phrases, there is a picture with a speech bubble containing the Italian. Underneath the picture is a guide to help you pronounce the Italian and an English translation. Like this:

Parlo italiano.

Parlo eetalee-ano.
I can speak Italian.

On the next two pages, you will find out how to use the pronunciation guide and there are some useful hints and phrases to remember. At the back of the book you can find some very basic Italian grammar, including a few common verbs.

Points to remember

We have not always had enough space to include the words for "please" (*per favore*), or "excuse me" (*mi scusi*). Try to remember to add them when you are asking for things.

Per favore.

There are four words in Italian for "you" – *tu, voi, Lei* and *Loro. Tu* (singular) and *voi* (plural) are used by close friends and children. *Lei* (singular) and *Loro* (plural) are for speaking to people you don't know very well. Be careful about using *tu* or *voi*, as people may think you are being rude.

Tu or Lei?

Pronunciation Guide

We have tried to keep the pronunciation guide in this book as simple as possible. For each Italian sound we have used the English word, or part of a word, which sounds most like it. Read the pronunciation guide in what seems to be the most obvious way. It will sound better if you say it quickly, so it is a good idea to practise a bit. People should be able to understand what you are saying, even if you won't sound quite like an Italian person. If you want to learn really good pronunciation you should try to find an Italian person to teach you.

Here are some general points to remember when you are trying to speak Italian.

Italian vowels are pronounced as follows:
"a" sounds like a mixture between the "a" sound in "ant" and "arm" in English.
"e" is either "e" as in "egg" or "ay" as in "day".
"i" is pronounced "ee" as in "keen".
"o" in the middle of a word is usually "o" as in "odd". At the end of a word it sounds like the "o" in nose.

Sometimes vowels have marks like these above them. These are called accents. They mean you should stress the vowel sound.

The letters "k", "w", "x" and "y" do not exist in Italian. "H" is used but it is never pronounced.

When a "c" comes before an "e" or an "i" it is pronounced "ch" as in "church". If it comes before an "a", an "o" or a "u", it is a hard sound as in "cake".

An "h" makes a "c" hard, even if it comes before an "e" or an "i".

When a "g" comes before an "e" or an "i", it is pronounced like the "j" in "jar". If it comes before an "a", an "o" or a "u" it is hard as in "games".

An "h" makes a "g" hard, even if it comes before an "e" or an "i".

The "r" is pronounced more clearly in Italian than it is in English. Think of the "r" in "grrr . . . !", the sound of a dog growling.

"Gl" is pronounced like the "lli" from our word "million".

"Gn" in Italian sounds like the "ni" part of the English word "onion".

"Qu" is pronounced "kw" as in the English word "quick".

C

ch

g

gh

r

gl

gn

qu

h

4

Some Basic Words and Phrases

Here are some useful words and phrases which you will need in all kinds of situations.

Sí	No
See	No
Yes	**No**
Per favore	Grazie
Pair favoray	Gratsee-ay
Please	**Thank you**

Buon giorno
Bwon jorno
Hello

Arrivederci
Arree-vedair-chee
Goodbye

Mi dispiace
Mee deespee-achay
I'm sorry

Mi scusi
Mee skoozee
Excuse me

Signore
Seenyoray
Mr

Signora
Seenyora
Mrs

Signorina
Seenyoreena
Miss

Some simple questions

How much?	Quanto?
	Kwanto?
Why?	Perché?
	Pairkay?
Which one?	Quale?
	Kwalay?
Where is . . . ?	Dov'è . . . ?
	Dovay . . . ?
When?	Quando?
	Kwando?
Have you . . . ?	Ha . . . ?
	A . . . ?
Is there . . . ?	C'è . . . ?
	Chay . . . ?
Are there . . . ?	Ci sono . . . ?
	Chee sono . . . ?

Some simple statements

I am . . .	Sono . . .
	Sono . . .
I have . . .	Ho . . .
	Oh . . .
It is . . .	È . . .
It is here.	Sta qui.
	Sta kwee.
It is there.	Sta lì.
	Sta lee.
This one.	Questo.
	Kwesto.
That one.	Quello.
	Kwello.
I would like . . .	Vorrei . . .
	Vorray . . .

Problems with the language

Do you speak English?
Parla eenglayzay?
Parla Inglese?

I do not speak Italian.
Non parlo eetalee-ano.
Non parlo italiano.

I do not understand.
Non kapeesko.
Non capisco.

Please speak more slowly.
Lenta-mentay, pair favoray.
Lentamente, per favore.

What does that mean?
Kay koza seen-yee-feeka?
Che cosa significa?

5

Finding your Way

Dov'è la stazione, per favore?

Dov'ay la statsee-onay, pair favoray?
How do I get to the railway station, please?

Devi prendere l'autobus numero cinque.

Dayvee prendairay l'owto-boos noomairo cheenkway.
You must take a number 5 bus.

Dov'è la fermata dell' autobus per il Colosseo?

Dov'ay la fairmata dell' owto-boos pair eel Coloss-ayo?
Where is the bus stop for the Colosseum?

È li. È quella.

Ay lee. Ay kwella.
Over there. It's that one.

Devo scendere qui per il Colosseo?

Dayvo shendairay kwee pair eel Coloss-ayo?
Is this where I get off for the Colosseum?

Per favore, dov'è il castello?

Pair favoray, dovay eel kastello?
Where is the castle, please?

Scusi. Mi sono perso. Come si chiama questa strada?

Skoozee. Mee sono pairso. Komay see kee-ama kwesta strada
Excuse me. I'm lost. What is the name of this street?

Mi può indicare sulla piantina?

Mee pwo eendee-karay soolla pee-anteena?
Can you show me on the map?

General directions

Girare a destra.
Jeeraray a destra.
Turn right.

Girare a sinistra.
Jeeraray a seeneestra.
Turn left.

Sempre diritto.
Sempray deereetto.
Go straight on.

È di fronte al cinema.
Ay dee frontay al cheenayma.
It's opposite the cinema.

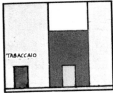

È accanto alla tabaccheria.
Ay akanto alla tabak-airee-a.
It's next to the tobacconists.

È all'angolo.
Ay al angolo.
It's on the corner.

È subito dopo il ponte.
Ay soobeeto dopo eel pontay.
It's just after the bridge.

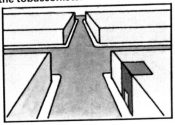

È prima dell'incrocio.
Ay preema dell eenkrocho.
It's just before the crossroads.

Some places to ask for

la stazione
la statsee-onay
railway station

l'aeroporto
l'airoporto
airport

il posto di polizia
eel posto dee poleetsee-a
police station

la banca
la banka
bank

i negozi
ee negotsee
the shops

7

At the Railway Station

Dove si comprano i biglietti?

Dovay see comprano ee beel-yetee?
Where can I buy a ticket?

Li, in fondo, alla biglietteria.

Lee, een fondo, alla beel-yettairee-a.
Over there, at the ticket office.

Quanto costa un biglietto per Roma?

Kwanto kosta oon beel-yetto pair Roma?
How much is it to Rome?

Un biglietto di andata per Roma.

Oon beel-yetto dee andata pair Roma.
One single ticket to Rome.

Due biglietti di andata e ritorno per Roma.

Doo-ay beel-yettee dee andata ay reetorno pair Roma.
Two return tickets to Rome

Da quale binario parte il treno per Roma?

Dal binario cinque.

Da kwalay beenaree-o partay eel trayno pair Roma?
Which platform does the Rome train leave from?

Dal beenaree-o cheenkway.
Platform five.

A che ora parte il treno?

A kay ora partay eel trayno?
What time does the train leave?

È questo il treno per Roma?

Ay kwesto eel trayno pair Roma?
Is this the Rome train?

Ho perso il mio biglietto!

O pairso eel mee-o beel-yetto!
I've lost my ticket!

A che ora arriva il treno da Venezia?

A kay ora arreeva eel trayno da Venetseea?
What time does the train from Venice arrive?

Facchino!

Fakeeno!
Porter!

Information

Luggage collection

Waiting room

Lost property

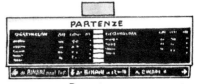

Departures

Left luggage

Not drinking water

It is dangerous to lean out of the window

9

Travelling by Car

Dovay see trova eel garaj pyoo veecheeno?
Where is the nearest garage?

Kwanta bentseena vwolay?
How much petrol do you want?

Eel pée-ayno, pair favoray.
Fill it up please.

Pwo controllaray l'olee-o ay l'akwa.
Can you check the oil and water?

La makeena ay gwasta.
I have broken down.

Kay koza soochayday?
What's the trouble?

Ee fraynee non foontsee-onamo baynay.
The brakes are not working properly.

Vorray nole-jaray oona makeena pair kwesta setteemana.
I would like to hire a car for the week.

Parts of the car

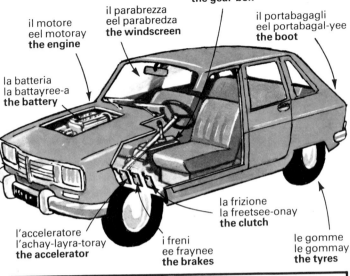

l'ingranaggio
l'eengranajo
the gear-box

il parabrezza
eel parabredza
the windscreen

il portabagagli
eel portabagal-yee
the boot

il motore
eel motoray
the engine

la batteria
la battayree-a
the battery

la frizione
la freetsee-onay
the clutch

l'acceleratore
l'achay-layra-toray
the accelerator

i freni
ee fraynee
the brakes

le gomme
le gommay
the tyres

Road signs

Danger of fire.

Beware of falling rocks.

Leave this entrance free.

Restricted parking area. You need a blue disc to park here.

Entrance to motorway.

Entrance to car park.

To city centre.

One way street.

At the Hotel

In Italy there are two main types of hotel, the *albergo,* and the *pensione,* which is less expensive. You can get lists of hotels from a tourist office, and at railway stations in large cities you can usually find an office which will find a hotel for you.

Booking in advance

Vorrei prenotare una camera per la settimana prossima.

Vorray prayno-taray oona kamayra pair la settee-mana prosseema.
I would like to book a room for next week.

Finding a room

Mi dispiace ma l'albergo è tutto completo.

Mee deespee-achay ma l'albairgo ay tootto completo.
I'm sorry but the hotel is full.

Mi può consigliare un altro albergo?

Mee pwo conseel-yaray oon altro albairgo?
Can you recommend another hotel?

Una camera a due letti.

Oona kamayra a doo-ay lettee.
A room with two beds.

Una camera a due letti con bagno.

Oona kamayra a doo-ay lettee con banyo.
A double room with bathroom.

Una camera singola con doccia.

Oona kamayra seengola con docha.
A single room with shower.

Per quanto tempo vi fermate qua?

Pair kwanto tempo vee fairmatay kwa?
How long will you be staying?

Hotel meals

Listino prezzi
Price list

Camera con prima colazione
Bed and breakfast

Mezza pensione
Half board

Pensione completa
Full board

A che ora si serve
la prima colazione
(il pranzo, la cena)?

A kay ora see sairvay
la preema kolatsee-onay
(eel prantso, la chayna)?
What time is breakfast (lunch, dinner) served?

Panini
Paneenee
Rolls

Burro
Boorro
Butter

Marmellata
Marmellata
Jam

Caffelatte
Kaffaylattay
White coffee

Mi può preparare un
cestino per il pranzo?

Mee pwo praypa-raray oon
chesteeno pair eel prantso?
**Could you make me a packed
lunch?**

La mia chiave,
per favore.

Qual'è il numero
della Sua camera?

La mee-a
kee-avay,
pair favoray.
**My key,
please.**

Kwalay eel
noomairo della
soo-a kamayra?
**What is your
room number?**

Voglio lasciare un
messaggio
per mio fratello.

Volyo lasharay oon messajo pair
mee-o fratello.
**I would like to leave a message for
my brother.**

Paying the bill

Mi può preparare il
conto, per favore?

Mee pwo pray-pararay eel konto,
pair favoray?
My bill, please.

13

Going Camping

There are many good campsites in Italy, both along the coast and inland. They often have good facilities, such as swimming pools and shops. You can get a list of approved sites from tourist offices.

Finding a campsite

Si può accamparsi qui?

See pwo akamparsee kwee?
May we camp here?

Scusi, c'è un campeggio qui vicino?

Skoozee, chay oon kampejo kwee veecheeno?
Is there a campsite near here?

Abbiamo una roulotte e due tende.

Abbee-amo oona roolottay ay doo-ay tenday.
We have a caravan and two tents.

At the campsite

Vogliamo fermarci per una settimana.

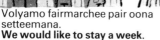

Volyamo fairmarchee pair oona setteemana.
We would like to stay a week.

Avete un posto all'ombra?

Avaytay oon posto all ombra?
Have you a place in the shade?

Ci sono altre famiglie inglesi qui?

Chee sono altray fameelyay eenglayzee kwee?
Are there any other English families here?

A che ora si chiude per la notte?

A kay ora see kee-ooday pair la nottay?
What time do you close in the evenings?

Dove posso lavarmi?

Dovay posso lavarmee?
Where can I wash?

Dov'è l'acqua?

Dovay l'akwa?
Where can I find some water?

Posso usare la Sua lampadina?

Posso oozaray la soo-a lampadeena?
May I borrow your torch?

Si può accendere un fuoco qui?

See pwo achend-ayray oon fwoko kwee?
Are you allowed to make a camp fire?

Che cos'è questa puzza?

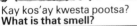

Kay kos'ay kwesta pootsa?
What is that smell?

Per favore, non potete fare meno rumore?

Pair favoray, non potaytay faray mayno roomoray?
Please could you make less noise?

What the signs mean

VIETATO LAVARE
I PIATTI
NEI LAVANDINI
No washing
up in the
basins

PARCHEGGIO OBBLIGATORIO
Compulsory parking

ACQUA
POTABILE
Drinking water

RISERVATO
ALLE
ROULOTTES
Caravans
only

SI PREGA DI
SERVIRSI DEI
BIDONI APPOSITI
Campers are
requested to
dispose of their
rubbish in the
provided places

Going Shopping

Most shops in Italy open from 9.00 a.m. to 7.30 p.m. They close for a long lunch, usually between 1.00 p.m. and 4.30 p.m. In most towns half day closing is on Wednesday.

Mi scusi, dove posso comprare della frutta?

Mee skoozee, dovay posso kompraray della froota? **Where can I buy some fruit?**

Ha delle mele?

A dellay maylay? **Have you any apples?**

Quante ne vuole?

Un chilo.

Kwantay nay vwolay? **How many would you like?**

Oon keelo. **A kilo.**

Quattro fette di prosciutto.

Kwattro fayttay dee proshootto. **Four slices of ham.**

Sto solo guardando.

Sto solo gwardando. **I am just looking.**

Signs

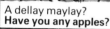

Saldi

Sale

Cassa

Pay here

ASCENSORE

Lift

APERTO DALLE 9 ALLE 18·30

Open from 9 a.m. to 6.30 p.m.

Buying clothes

Mi può aiutare?
Cerco una camicia
a disegni.

Sì. Quale
misura desidera?

Mee pwo eye-ootaray?
Chairko oona kameecha
a deesayn-yee.
**Can you help me? I am looking
for a patterned shirt.**

See. Kwalay meesoora
dayseedaira?
Yes. What size do you want.

Posso provarla?

Posso provarla?
May I try it on?

È troppo
grande.

È troppo
piccola.

Ay troppo
granday.
**It's too
big.**

Ay troppo
peekola.
**It's too
small.**

Quant'è?

Kwant'ay?
How much is it?

Ha qualcosa
meno cara?

A kwalkoza mayno karo?
Have you anything cheaper?

Dove si paga?

Dovay see paga?
Where do I pay?

Grazie.

Prego.

Gratsee-ay.
Thank you.

Praygo.
You are welcome.

The Shops 1

Alimentari

Aleemen-taree **Grocers**

Vorrei . . .

Vorray . . .
I would like . . .

delle conserve
dellay konsairvay
some tinned foods

formaggio
formajo
cheese

burro
boorro
butter

uova
wova
eggs

marmellata
marmellata
jam

té
tay
tea

zucchero
zookairo
sugar

biscotti
beeskottee
biscuits

miele
mee-aylay
honey

senape
senapay
mustard

latte
lattay
milk

fagioli
fajolee
green beans

piselli
peesellee
peas

caffé
kaffay
coffee

funghi
foongee
mushrooms

cavolfiore
kavolfee-oray
cauliflower

patate
patatay
potatoes

lattuga
lattooga
lettuce

lamponi
lamponee
raspberries

cavolo
kavolo
cabbage

pomodori
pomodoree
tomatoes

cipolle
cheepollay
onions

un limone
oon leemonay
a lemon

mele
maylay
apples

pere
payray
pears

un'arancia
oon arancha
an orange

delle susine
dellay sooseenay
plums

fragole
fragolay
strawberries

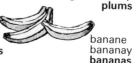

banane
bananay
bananas

MACELLERIA

Machellaire-a
Butcher

manzo tritato
mantso treetato
minced beef

un pollo
oon pollo
a chicken

un bistecca
oona beestayka
a steak

scaloppine di vitello
skaloppeenay dee veetello
escalop of veal

Salumeria

Saloom-airee-a
Pork butcher

antipasti vari
anteepastee varee

prosciutto di
Parma

salsicce
salseechay
sausages

proshootto dee
Parma
Parma ham

salame
salamay
salami

prepared salads
and cooked
meats

PANIFICIO

Panee-feecho
Baker

dei panini
day-ee paneenee
some rolls

pane
panay
bread

un filone
oon feelonay
a long loaf

PASTICCERIA

Pasteechairee-a
Cake and sweet shop

una torta di frutta
oona torta dee frootta
a fruit tart

delle caramelle
dellay kara-mellay
some sweets

una pasta
oona pasta
a cake

PESCHERIA

Peskairee-a
Fishmonger

sogliola
sol-yola
sole

nasello
nazello
hake

un gambero
oon gambairo
a prawn

merluzzo
mairlootzo
cod

The Shops 2

Libreria-Cartoleria-Edicola

Leebrair-reeya – Kartolaireeya – Edeekola
Bookshop – Stationers – Newspaper kiosk

inchiostro
eenkee-ostro
ink

una biro
oona beero
a biro

un giornale
oon jornalay
a newspaper

un libro
oon leebro
a book

una gomma
oona gomma
a rubber

una matita
oona mateeta
a pencil

delle buste
dellay boostay
envelopes

TABACCHERIA

Tabak-airee-a
Tobacconist

carta da lettere
karta da lettairay
writing paper

un pacchetto di sale
oon paketto dee salay
a packet of salt

un pacchetto di sigarette
oon paketto dee seega-rettay
a packet of cigarettes

fiammiferi
fee-ammee-fairee
matches

francobolli
franko-bollee
stamps

Abbigliamento

Abbeelya-mento
Clothes shop

un cappello
oon kappello
a hat

una camicia
oona kameecha
a shirt

dei calzoni corti
day-ee kaltsonee kortee
shorts

un vestito
oon vesteeto
a dress

una gonna
oona gonna
a skirt

delle scarpe
dellay skarpay
some shoes

dei sandali
day-ee sandalee
some sandals

un maglione
oon malyee-onay
a jersey

dei pantaloni
day-ee pantalonee
trousers

un costume da bagno
oon kostoomay da banyo
a bathing costume

un impermeabile
oon eempairmay-abeelay
a raincoat

20

FERRAMENTA

Ferramenta
Ironmongers – hardware store

un apriscatole
oon apree-skatolay
a tin opener

un cacciavite
oon kacha-veetay
a screwdriver

un cavatappi
oon kava-tappee
a corkscrew

spago
spago
string

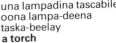
una lampadina tascabile
oona lampa-deena
taska-beelay
a torch

una pila
oona peela
a battery

una lampadina elettrica
oona lampa-deena ele-ttreeka
a light bulb

detersivo
deterseevo
detergent

forbici
forbeechee
scissors

filo
feelo
cotton

un ago
oon ago
a needle

una spina
oona speena
a plug

una bombolina di gas
oona bombo-leena
dee gaz
Camping gas

FARMACIA

Farmachee-a
Chemist

aspirine
aspee-reenay
aspirins

una benda
oona benda
a bandage

insetticida
eensettee-cheeda
insecticide

sapone
saponay
soap

talco
talko
talcum powder

dentifricio
dentee-freechee-o
toothpaste

uno spazzolino da
denti
oono spatso-leeno
da dentee
a toothbrush

una pellicola
oona pellee-kola
a film

dei cerotti
day chairottee
sticking plaster

un pettine
con petteenay
a comb

della carta igenica
della karta eejay-neeka
a roll of toilet paper

21

Posting a Letter . . .

The post office is called *ufficio postale*. They are usually open from 8.15 a.m. to 2.00 p.m. You can also buy stamps from a *tabaccheria*. There are letter boxes in the streets as well as at post offices. If you are posting letters abroad make sure you use a box marked *estero*.

Scusi. Quanto è per l'Inghilterra.

Skoozee. Kwanto ay pair l'Eengeel-terra?
Excuse me. How much is it to England?

Vorrei quattro francobolli per l'Inghilterra.

Vorray kwattro franko-bolee pair l'Eengeel-terra.
I would like four stamps to England.

Mi scusi. Dov'è una cassetta postale?

Mee skoozee. Dovay oona kassetta postalay?
Excuse me, where can I find a postbox.

The post office

Dov'è l'ufficio postale?

Dovay l'oofeecho postalay?
Where is the post office?

Voglio mandare un telegramma in Inghilterra.

Volyo mandaray oon telegramma een Eengeel-terra.
I would like to send a telegram to England.

Compili questo modulo, per favore.

Compeelee kwesto modoolo, pair favoray.
Fill in this form, please.

Quanto costa per parola?

Kwanto kosta pair parola?
How much is it per word?

. . . and Changing Money

Quanto costa spedire questo pacco in Inghilterra?

Kwanto kosta spedeeray kwesto pako een Eengeel-terra?
How much will it cost to send this parcel to England?

A che ora è l'ultima raccolta delle lettere?

A kay ora ay l'oolteema rackolta dellay lettairay?
What times does the last post leave?

Signs

PER VIA AEREA

Air mail

Pacchi

Parcels

TELEGRAMMI

Telegrams

FRANCOBOLLI

Postage stamps

Changing money

You can change money and traveller's cheques in a bank, a *cambio* (exchange office) and in some railway stations and hotels. Remember to take your passport with you. Banks are usually open from 8.30 a.m. to 1.30 p.m., but exchange offices are open for longer.

Scusi. Cambiate i travellers cheques?

Skoozee. Kambee-atay ee traveller's cheques?
Excuse me. Do you cash traveller's cheques?

Quanto vale la sterlina?

Kwanto valay la stairleena?
How many lira are there to the pound?

Scusi. Posso avere degli spiccioli?

Skoozee. Posso avairay dayl-yee speecholee?
Could I have some small change?

Going to a Bar

Bars in Italy stay open for much of the day. You can buy snacks and both alcoholic and soft drinks. Often you pay more to sit down, and if you stand you must usually pay for your drink before ordering from the barman.

È occupata questa tavola?

Ay okoo-pata kwesta tavola?
Is this table taken?

Che cosa desiderano?

Kay koza daysee-dairano?
What can I get you?

Possiamo vedere il menù?

Possee-amo vayd-airay eel maynoo?
Please may we see the menu.

Che tipo di panini avete?

Prosciutto, formaggio e salame.

Kay teepo dee paneenee avaytay?
What sandwiches have you got?
Proshootto, formajo ay salamay.
Ham, cheese and salami.

Vorrei due panini con prosciutto, una coca-cola e un'aranciata.

Vorray doo-ay paneenee con proshootto, oona coco-cola ay con 'aranchata.
I would like two ham sandwiches, a coca cola and an orangeade.

Una forchetta, per favore.

Oona forketta, pair favoray.
A fork, please.

Non ho ordinato questo.

Non o ordeenato kwesto.
I didn't order this.

Un coltello

Oon koltello
A knife

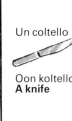

Un cucchiaio
Oon kookee-eye-o
A spoon

Un tovagliolo
Oon toval-yee-olo
A napkin

Una brocca di acqua

Oona brokka dee akwa
A jug of water

Un bicchiere
Oon beekee-airay
A glass

Sale e pepe
salay ay paypay
Sale and pepper

Dove sono i gabinetti?

Dovay sono ee gabee-nettee?
Where are the toilets?

Cameriere!

Kamairee-airay!
Waiter!

Il conto, per favore.

Eel konto, pair favoray.
The bill, please.

È compreso il servizio?

Ay comprayso eel sairveetsee-o?
Is service included?

Going to a Restaurant

In Italy there are different types of restaurant. The more expensive are called *Ristoranti,* but *Trattorie* offer good food at reasonable prices. Look out for restaurants with a *Menu Turistico,* a fixed price meal.

Vorrei prenotare una tavola per quattro persone alle otto.

Vorray praynotaray oona tavola pair kwattro personay allay otto.
I would like to book a table for four at 8 p.m.

Avete una tavola per quattro?

Avaytay oona tavola pair kwattro?
Have you a table for four?

Ha prenotato?

A prayno-tato?
Have you booked?

Avete una tavola fuori?

Avaytay oona tavola fworee?
Have you a table outside?

Che cosa desiderano?

Kay koza dayzeed-airano?
What would you like to order?

Come si fa questo piatto?

Komay see fa kewsto pee-atto?
How is this dish made?

Avete qualcosa di più semplice?

Avaytay kwalkoza pyoo dee sempleechay?
Have you got anything plainer?

Drinks

Posso vedere la lista dei vini?

Posso vaydairay la leesta dayee veenee?
Could I see the wine list?

Che cosa mi consiglia?

Kay koza mee conseel-ya?
What do you recommend?

Vorrei una bottiglia di vino da tavola e una bottiglia di acqua minerale.

Vorray oona botteel-ya dee veeno da tavola ay oona botteel-ya dee akwa mineralay.
I would like a bottle of table wine and a bottle of mineral water.

Quali analcoolici avete?

Kwalee analko-oleechee avaytay?
What soft drinks have you got?

Mi dispiace, ho rovesciato il bicchiere.

Mee deespee-achay, o roveshato eel beekee-airay.
I'm sorry, I've spilt my drink.

Abbiamo un po' di fretta.

Abbee-amo oon po dee fretta.
We are in a bit of a hurry.

Problems with the bill

Mi scusi. Che vuol dire questo?

Mee skoozee. Kay vwol deeray kwesto?
Excuse me. What does this mean?

27

The Menu

un panino
oon paneeno
a sandwich

un tost
oon tost
a toasted sandwich

una pasta
oona pasta
a cake

una pizza
oona peetsa
a pizza

formaggio
formajo
cheese

Le bevande
Lay bayvanday
Drinks

un cappuccino
oon kapoocheeno
white coffee

un caffe
oon kaffay
a black coffee

un té
oon tay
a cup of tea

un'aranciata
oon 'aranchata
an orangeade

un bicchiere di
latte
oon beekee-
airay dee lattay
a glass of milk

Restaurant menu

Look out for restaurants which have a special set menu called
a *Menu a prezzo fisso* or *Menu turistico*. It is cheaper to have this
type of meal than to choose from an ordinary menu. *Vino compreso*
means that wine is included in the price. All Italian restaurants
(except a Tavola Calda, where you sit at a bar) have a cover charge
(*coperto*).

La Lista del Giorno
Today's Menu
Antipasti

salame
salamay
salami

prosciutto
proshootto
ham

Starters

uova alla maionese
wova alla my-yonaysay
egg mayonnaise

olive
oleevay
olives

sott'oli
sott'olee
**pickled
vegetables**

Primi piatti
First course

spaghetti al pomodoro
spagettee al pomo-doro
spaghetti in tomato sauce

minestrone
meene-stronay
minestrone soup

risotto alla pescatora
reesotto alla peska-tora
risotto with seafood

tagliatelle alla panna
tall-yatellay alla panna
noodles in cream

LA PASTASCIUTTA
La pasta-shootta
Types of pasta

gli spaghetti
l-yee
spagettee
spaghetti

i ravioli
ee ravee-olee
ravioli

i maccheroni
ee makair-onee
macaroni

i rigatoni
ee reega-tonee
rigatoni

i tortellini
ee tortel-leenee
tortellini

le lasagne
lay lazanyay
lasagna

i fusilli
ee foozeelee
fusili

le farfalle
lay farfallay
'butterflies'

le tagliatelle
lay tallya-tellay
tagliatelle

le stelline
lay stelleenay
little stars

il parmigiano
eel parmee-jano
parmesan cheese

---

fritto misto
freetto meesto
mixed fried fish

Pesce
Fish

trota all griglia
trota alla greel-ya
grilled trout

Secondi piatti
Second course

pollo arrosto
pollo arrosto
roast chicken

una bistecca
oona beesteka
a steak

stufato
stoofato
beef stew

ossobuco
osso-booko
shin of veal

agnello al forno
anyello al forno
roast lamb

Contorni

patate fritte
patatay freettay
chips

Vegetables

fagioli
fajolee
beans

insalata mista
eensalata meesta
mixed salad

Frutta
Fruit

Dolce
Sweet

Formaggio
Cheese

Entertainments 1

To find out what is on in the area, look in a local paper, or ask at the nearest Tourist Office (*Ente del Turismo*). If you are staying in a hotel, the receptionist may be able to help. Some cinemas have films outside in summer.

C'è qualche buono spettacolo da vedere?

Chay kwalkay bwono spettacolo da vedairay?
Can you recommend a show to see?

Circo
Cherko
Circus

Teatro dei burattini
Tay-atro dayee boora-tteenee
Puppet theatre

Un cartone animato
Oon kartonay aneemato
Cartoon film

Teatro all'aperto
Tay-atro all'apairto
Open-air theatre

Un lunapark
Oon loonapark
A fairground

Una pantomima
Oona panto-meema
A pantomime

Uno spettacolo storico
Oono spettakolo storiko
A Pageant
(A play which illustrates the history of a place.)

Un mago
Oon mago
A magician

Una partita di calcio
Oona parteeta dee kalcho
A football match

Che c'è stasera al cinema?

Kay chay stasaira al cheenema?
What is on at the cinema?

C'è un film in Inglese?

Chay oon feelm een Eenglaysay?
Is there a film in English?

Quanto costa?

Kwanto kosta?
How much are the tickets?

Due posti in platea.

Doo-ay postee een platay-a.
Two seats in the stalls.

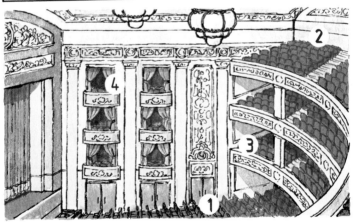

1 La platea
La platay-a
The stalls

2 Il loggione
Eel lojonay
The gods

3 La galleria
La gallairee-a
The dress circle

4 I palchi
Ee palkee
Boxes

Entertainments 2

A kay ora komeencha
lo spetta-kolo?
What time does the show begin?

Allay settay ay medzo.
Feeneeshay allay otto.
At six thirty p.m. It finishes at eight p.m.

Dovay posso kompraray oon
programma?
Where can I buy a programme?

La maskaira lee venday.
The usherette sells them.

Theatre signs

Cloakroom

Fire exit

Toilets

No smoking

The sign means that children under the age of 18 are not allowed to see the show.

Sightseeing 1

The *Ente del Turismo* will also give you sightseeing information. You will sometimes have to pay an entrance fee to visit places of interest. Most museums are closed on Monday, and others on some afternoons as well. Be sure to check in advance.

Che c'è di interessante da vedere in città?

Kay chay dee eenteress-antay da vedairay een cheetta?
What is there of interest to see in the town?

Places to go sightseeing

Il castello
Eel kastello
The castle

il giardino zoologico
Eel jardeeno zo-olojeeko
The zoo

Il museo
Eel moozayo
The museum

La chiesa
La kee-ayza
The church

Il centro storico
Eel chentro storeeko
Old part of town

Parco nazionale
Parko natsee-onalay
National park

Le grotte
Lay grottay
Caves

C'è una pianta turistica della città?

Chay oona pee-anta tooreest-eeka della cheetta?
Is there a tourist map of the town?

Mi può dire quando è aperto il museo?

Mee pwo deeray kwando ay apairto eel moozayo?
Can you tell me when the museum is open?

Ogni giorno, tranne il lunedì, dalle nove all'una.

On-yee jorno, trannay eel loonaydee, dallay novay all oona.
Every day, except Monday, from 9 a.m. to 1 p.m.

Quanto è l'ingresso?

Kwanto ay L'eengresso?
How much is the admission charge?

Sightseeing 2

Guided tours

Chay oona veezeeta con
gweeda eenglayzay?
Is there a guided tour in English?

See. La prosseema veezeeta
komincha fra oon kwarto d'oro.
**Yes. The next tour starts in a
quarter of an hour.**

Kwanto doora la veezeeta?
How long does the tour last?

See pwo saleeray soolla torray?
Can one go up the tower?

At the zoo

I rettili
Ee retteelee
Reptile house

L'uccelliera
L'oochellee-aira
The aviary

Le scimmie
Lay sheemee-ay
Monkey house

La merenda degli scimpanze
La mairenda dayl-yee
sheempantsay
Chimpanzees Tea Party

La fossa degli orsi
La fossa day-lyee orsee
Bear pit

Un giro sull'asino
Oon jeero sool azeeno
Donkey rides

Un giro sul cammello
Oon jeero sool
kammello
Camel rides

34

Signs

Do not feed
the Animals

Dangerous
Animals

Wild Animals

Entrance

Exit

Do not Touch

Cameras Prohibited

Restaurant

Private Property

Beward of
the Dog

No Entrance

Closed for
the Holidays

Open

Closed

Keep off
the Grass

Making Friends

Chow. Komay tee kee-amee?
Hello. What is your name?

Mee kee-amee Maree-a. Ay too?
My name is Maria. And yours?

Dovay abeetee?
Where are you staying?

Abito lajjoo.
I live over there.

Kwantee annee eye?
How old are you?

O dodeechee annee.
I'm 12.

Kwesto ay mee-o fratello, Marco. Eye day fratellee?
This is my brother, Marco. Have you any brothers or sisters?

See. O oona sorella pyoo granday. Ay kwesto ay eel mee-o jemello.
Yes. I have an elder sister. And here is my twin brother.

Puoi mangiare con noi?

Pwoy manjaray kon noy?
Can you have lunch with us?

Devo chiedere ai miei genitori.

Devo kee-aydairay eye mee-ay jeneetoray.
I must ask my parents.

Andiamo a giocare!

Andee-amo a jokaray!
Let's go and play!

Fate presto!

Vengo!

Aspettami!

Fatay presto!
Hurry up!

Vengo!
I'm coming!

Aspetta-mee!
Wait for me!

Mi piace . . .

Mee pee-achay . . .
I like . . .

Gli Scacchi
L-yee Skackee
Chess

Dipingere
Deepeen-jairay
Painting

La Filatelia
La Feela-taylee-a
Stamp collecting

Cards

Le Carte
Lay Kartay

Quadri
Kwadree
Diamonds

Cuori
Koo-oree
Hearts

Fiori
Fee-oree
Clubs

Picche
Peekay
Spades

Il re
Eel ray
King

La regina
La rayjeena
Queen

Il fante
Eel fantay
Jack

L'asso
L'asso
Ace

Il jolly
Eel jollee
Joker

Playing Games

L'altalena
L'alta-layna
Swing

Buttami la palla!

Tieni!

Bocttammee la palla!
Throw me the ball!

Tee-aynee!
Catch!

Nascondiglio
Naskondeel-yo
Hide and seek

Cavallina
Kavalleena
Leap frog

A che cosa giocate?

Si chiamano le bocce.

See kee-amano lay bochay.
It's called bocce.

A kay koza jokatay?
What are you playing?

Sports

There is a lot of good fishing in Italy, especially in the mountains. To find out if you need a permit for the area you are in, ask at the Town Hall, *Il Comune.* They will issue you with a *Permesso di Pesca,* or direct you to the owner of the river.

Going fishing

Dove posso noleggiare una canna da pesca?

Dovay posso nolejaray oona kanna da peska?
Where can I hire a fishing rod?

Quanto costa al giorno?

Kwanto costa al jorno?
How much does it cost for the day?

Bisogna avere un permesso?

Beesonya avairay oon pairmesso?
Must one have a permit?

Ha dell'esca, per favore?

A dell'eska, pair favoray?
Have you any bait, please?

È un buon posto per pescare?

Ay oon bwon posto pair peskaray?
Is this a good place to fish?

Riding

Si può cavalcare qui vicino?

See pwo kaval-karay kwee veecheeno?
Can one go riding near here?

Vogliamo delle lezioni di equitazione.

Vol-yamo dellay leztsee-onee dee ekwee-tatsee-onay.
We would like some riding lessons.

Skiing

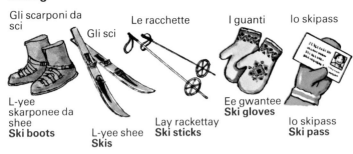

Gli scarponi da sci
L-yee skarponee da shee
Ski boots

Gli sci
L-yee shee
Skis

Le racchette
Lay rackettay
Ski sticks

I guanti
Ee gwantee
Ski gloves

lo skipass
lo skipass
Ski pass

Dov'è la scuola di sci?

Dov'ay la skoo-ola dee shee?
Where is the ski school?

The ski runs

The ski runs, or Piste, are marked with coloured arrows.

Nursery slopes – very easy.

Beginners – easy.

For quite experienced skiers – quite difficult.

For professional skiers – very difficult.

Sono un principiante.

Sono oon preenchee-pee-antay.
I am a beginner.

Ho già sciato una volta.

O jar shee-ato oona volta.
I have skied once before.

So sciare bene.

So shee-aray baynay.
I can ski well.

Non posso alzarmi. Mi può aiutare?

Non posso altsarmee. Mee pwo eye-ootaray?
I cannot get up. Can you help me?

Ci siamo persi. Dov'è la sciovia?

Chee see-amo pairso. Dov'ay la shee-ovee-a?
We are lost. Where is the ski-lift?

At the Seaside 1

Dov'è la spiaggia più vicina?

Dov'ay la spee-ajay pyoo veecheena?
Where is the nearest beach?

C'è una piscina?

Chay oona peesheena?
Is there a swimming pool?

Vorrei noleggiare due sedie a sdraio . . .

Vorray nole-jaray doo-ay saydee-ay a sdry-yo . . .
I would like to hire two deck chairs

. . . e un ombrellone.

. . . ay oon ombrellonay.
. . . and a parasol.

Dove posso cambiarmi?

Accanto alla piscina per bambini.

Dove posso kambee-armee?
Where are the changing rooms?
Accanto alla peesheena pair bambeenee.
Next to the paddling pool.

Beach things

Un salvagente
Oon salva-jentay

Un canotto
Oon canotto

Una palla
Oona palla

Un materassino
Oon materasseeno

Crema solare
Krayma solaray

Ciao. Andiamo a fare un bagno?

Chow. Andee-amo a faray oon banyo? **Hello. Let's go for a swim.**

Può badare alla mia roba, per favore?

Pwo badaray alla mee-a roba, pair favoray? **Please could you look after my things for me?**

Attenzione! Arriva un'onda grande!

Attentsee-onay! Arreeva oon onda granday! **Watch out! There's a big wave coming!**

C'è una doccia?

Chay oona docha? **Is there a shower?**

Passami l'asciugamano.

Passamee l'ashooga-mano. **Pass me the towel.**

Lo sci nautico
Lo shee nowtiko
Water skiing

Pedalò
Pedalo
Pedalo

Una barca a vela
Oona barca a vayla
Sailing boat

At the Seaside 2

Facciamo un castello di sabbia?

Hai un secchiello e una paletta?

Fachamo oon kastello dee sabbee-a?
Shall we build a sand castle?
Eye oon seckee-ello ay oona paletta?
Have you got a bucket and spade?

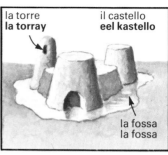

la torre
la torray
il castello
eel kastello

la fossa
la fossa

Che cosa significa la bandiera rossa?

Kay koza seenyee-feeka la bandee-aira rossa?
What does the red flag mean?

È pericoloso fare il bagno. Il mare è mosso.

VIETATO FARE IL BAGNO

Ay payree-kolozo faray eel banyo. Eel maray ay mosso.
It is dangerous to swim. The sea is too rough.

No bathing

Ho caldo.

O kaldo.
I'm hot.

Andiamo a comprare un gelato.

Andee-amo a kompraray oon jelato.
Let's go and buy an ice cream.

44

Buying an ice cream

Per favore, ha dei gelati?

Pair favoray, a day-ee jelatee?
Excuse me, do you have any ice creams?

GELATI

Sì. Quale gusto?

See. Kwalay goosto?
Yes. What flavour would you like?

 Crema
Krayma
Vanilla

Fragola
Fragola
Strawberry

 Panna
Panna
Cream

Nocciola
Nochola
Nutty

 Pistacchio
Peestacho
Pistachio

Cioccolato
Chokolato
Chocolate

Voglio un gelato alla crema.

Volyo oon jelato alla krayma.
I would like a vanilla ice cream.

Normale o doppio?

Un ghiacciolo grande alla fragola.

Normalay o doppee-o?
A single or a double?

Oon gee-acholo granday alla fragola.
A large strawberry lolly.

Quant'è?

Kwant'ay?
How much is it?

Trecento lire.

Grazie.

Traychento leeray.
Three hundred lira.

Gratsee-ay.
Thank you.

Accidents and Emergencies

You can find the numbers for fire, police and ambulance services on the first page of the telephone directory (*elenco telefonico*). Road accidents should be reported to the police (*la polizia*). If you are in serious trouble, contact the British Consulate.

Aiuto!

Eye-ooto!
Help!

Venite subito!

Veneetay soobeeto!
Come quickly!

Fuoco!

Fwoko!
Fire!

Per favore, chiamate un'ambulanza.

Pair favoray, kee-amatay oon' amboolantsa.
Please call for an ambulance.

Missing persons

Il mio amico manca da ieri sera.

Ell mee-o ameeko manka da ee-airee saira.
My friend has been missing since last night.

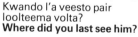

Quando l'ha visto per l'ultima volta?

Kwando l'a veesto pair loolteema volta?
Where did you last see him?

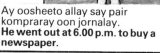

È uscito alle sei per comprare un giornale.

Ay oosheeto allay say pair kompraray oon jornalay.
He went out at 6.00 p.m. to buy a newspaper.

Portava un cappello rosso e un sciarpa.

Portava con kapello rosso ay oon sharpa.
He was wearing a red hat and scarf.

Lost or stolen

Ho perso il mio passaporto.

O pairso eel mee-o passaporto.
I have lost my passport.

Mi hanno rubato il portafoglio.

Mee anno roobato eel portafolyo.
My wallet has been stolen.

Mi hanno svaligiato la camera.

Me anno svalee-jato la kamaira.
My room has been burgled.

Dove possiamo metterci in contatto con Lei?

Dovay possee-yamo mettairchee een kontatto con lay?
Where can we contact you?

Other things

i miei traveller's cheques.
ee mee-ayee traveller's cheques
my traveller's cheques

la mia macchina fotografica
la mee-a makeena fotograf-eeka
my camera

la mia valigia
la mee-a valleeja
my suitcase

le mie chiavi
lay mee-ay kee-avee
my keys

la mia borsa
la mee-a borsa
my bag

il mio orologio
eel mee-o orolojo
my watch

È successo fra le dieci e mezzogiorno.

Ay soochesso fra le dee-aychee ay metsojorno.
It happened between 10.00 p.m. and midday.

Ecco il mio nome e il mio indirizzo.

Ecko eel mee-o nomay ay eel mee-o eendee-reedzo.
Here is my name and address.

47

Using the Telephone

In Italy you can find public telephones in most bars, or you could look for a telephone box, or *cabina telefonica*.

Some telephones are only for local calls. If you want to call out of town, look for the sign *teleselezione* or *interurbano*. To make a long distance or overseas call you should go to a large post office or telephone exchange (*S.I.P.*).

To use a call box you need a special token called a *gettone*. You can buy these from a *tabaccheria* or get them from a machine in a call box.

When you make a call first put in the *gettone* (one for a local call, six for elsewhere), then lift the receiver and dial the number.

This sign outside a bar shows that the bar has a public telephone.

Put your *gettone* in here.

Press this button to get unused *gettoni* back.

Posso usare il telefono?

Posso oozaray eel telefono?
Please may I use the telephone?

Per favore, mi puo dare dei gettoni?

Pair favoray, mee pwo daray day-ee jetonee?
Please could you give me some telephone tokens?

Making a phone call

Voglio fare una chiamata "erre" a Londra. Il numero è Londra....

Volyo faray oona kee-amata "erray" a Londra. Eel noomairo ay Londra...
I want to call London and reverse the charges. The number is London ...

Qual'è il suo numero? Un attimo, prego.

Kwal'ay eel soo-o noomairo? Oon atteemo, praygo.
What is your number? hold the line.

Ha sbagliato numero.

A sbal-yato noomairo.
Wrong number.

Pronto! Posso parlare con il signor Rossi?

Pronto! Posso parlaray con eel Seenyor Rossi?
Please may I speak to Mr Rossi?

Il numero è occupato.

Eel noomairo ay ockoopato.
The number is engaged.

Non è qui in questo momento.

Non ay kwee een kwesto momento.
He is not here at the moment.

Chi parla?

Kee parla?
Who is speaking?

Può dirgli che ha telefonato la signora Brown, e che mi può richiamare a questo numero.

Pwo deerl-yee kay a telefontato la seenyora Brown, ay kay mee pwo reekee-amaray a kwesto noomairo.
Could you tell him that Mrs Brown telephoned, and ask him to ring at this number.

49

Feeling Ill

The *farmacia* will be able to give you advice and medicines for most minor ailments. If you see a doctor, you may have to pay him on the spot. In case of emergency, ask for *pronto soccorso*.

Ho mal di testa.
O mal dee testa.
I have a headache.

Ho mal di stomaco.
O mal dee stomako.
I have a stomach-pain.

Ho il raffreddore.
O eel raffreddoray.
I have a cold.

Tossisco molto.
Tossisko molto.
I am coughing a lot.

Ho la febbre.
O la febbray.
I have a temperature.

Ho la nausea.
O la nowzaya.
I feel sick.

Mi sono tagliato.
Mee sono tal-yato.
I have cut myself.

Mi sono bruciato.
Mee sono broochato.
I have burnt myself.

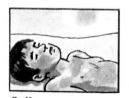

Soffro
d'insolazione.
Soffro d'eenso-
latsee-onay.
I am suffering from sunstroke.

Mi ha punto/morso . . .
Mee a poonto/morso . . .
I have been stung/bitten by . . .

una medusa
oona medoosa
a jellyfish

un riccio
oon reecho
a sea-urchin

un serpente
oon sairpenta
a snake

una vespa
oona vespa
a wasp

50

Ho qualcosa
nell'occhio.
O kwalkoza nell
ockee-o.
**I have something in
my eye.**

Ho uno sfogo.
O oono sfogo.
I have a rash.

Mi pizzica.
Mee peetseeka.
It itches.

Ho mal di denti.
O mal dee dentee.
I have toothache.

Mi ha morso un cane.
Mee a morso oon
kanay.
**I have been bitten
by a dog.**

Mi sono rotto la
gamba.
Mee sono rotto la
gamba.
I have broken my leg.

Going to the doctor

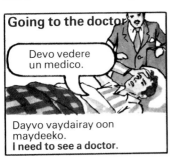

Devo vedere
un medico.

Dayvo vaydairay oon
maydeeko.
I need to see a doctor.

Quando sarà libero?

Kwando sara leebairo?
When is he free?

Mi può vaccinare
contro il tetano?

Mee pwo vacheen-aray kontro
eel tetano?
**Can you innoculate me against
tetanus?**

Mi può dare una
ricetta medica?

Mee pwo daray oona reechetta
maydeeka?
Can you give me a prescription.

Parts of the Body

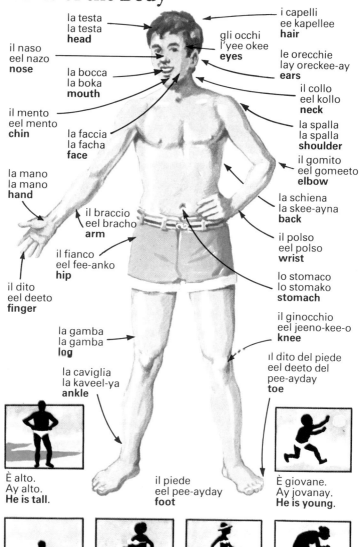

la testa
la testa
head

i capelli
ee kapellee
hair

gli occhi
l'yee okee
eyes

il naso
eel nazo
nose

le orecchie
lay oreckee-ay
ears

la bocca
la boka
mouth

il collo
eel kollo
neck

il mento
eel mento
chin

la spalla
la spalla
shoulder

la faccia
la facha
face

il gomito
eel gomeeto
elbow

la mano
la mano
hand

la schiena
la skee-ayna
back

il braccio
eel bracho
arm

il polso
eel polso
wrist

il fianco
eel fee-anko
hip

lo stomaco
lo stomako
stomach

il dito
eel deeto
finger

il ginocchio
eel jeeno-kee-o
knee

la gamba
la gamba
leg

il dito del piede
eel deeto del
pee-ayday
toe

la caviglia
la kaveel-ya
ankle

il piede
eel pee-ayday
foot

È alto.
Ay alto.
He is tall.

È giovane.
Ay jovanay.
He is young.

È basso.
Ay basso.
He is short.

È grassa.
Ay grassa.
She is fat.

È magra.
Ay magra.
She is thin.

È vecchia.
Ay veckee-a.
She is old.

Colours

Colori (Koloree)

nero
nayro
black

bianco
bee-anko
white

grigio
greejo
grey

beige
bayj
beige

marrone
marronay
brown

giallo
jallo
yellow

arancio
arancho
orange

rosso
rosso
red

rosa
roza
pink

viola
vee-ola
violet

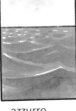

azzurro
adzoorro
blue

verde
vairday
green

oro
oro
gold

argento
arjento
silver

scuro
skooro
dark

chiaro
kee-aro
light

Months, Seasons and Days

Gennaio
Jen-eye-yo
January

Febbraio
Febr-eye-yo
February

Marzo
Martso
March

Aprile
Apreelay
April

Maggio
Majo
May

Giugno
Jyoonyo
June

Luglio
Loolyo
July

Agosto
Agosto
August

Settembre
Settembray
September

Ottobre
Ottobray
October

Novembre
Novembray
November

Dicembre
Deechembray
December

Days of the week

7 Lunedì
Loonaydee
Monday

8 Martedì
Martaydee
Tuesday

9 Mercoledì
Maircolaydee
Wednesday

10 Giovedì
Jovaydee
Thursday

11 Venerdì
Vaynairdee
Friday

12 Sabato
Sabato
Saturday

13 Domenica
Domayneeka
Sunday

The seasons

La primavera
La preemavaira
The spring

L'estate
L'estatay
The summer

L'autunno
L'owtoono
The autumn

L'inverno
L'eenvairno
The winter

The Weather

Il Tempo
Eel Tempo

Piove.
Peeyovay.
It's raining.

Sta per piovere.
Sta pair peeyovairay.
It's going to rain.

Grandina.
Grandeena.
It's hailing.

Tira vento.
Teera vento.
It's windy.

Nevica.
Nayveeka.
It's snowing.

È nuvoloso.
Ay noovoloso.
It's cloudy.

Tuona.
Twona.
It's thundering.

Un lampo.
Oon lampo.
A flash of lightning.

Fa fresco.
Fa fresco.
It's cool.

È una bella giornata.
Ay oona bella jornata.
It's a nice day.

Fa caldo.
Fa kaldo.
It's hot.

Fa freddo.
Fa freddo.
It's cold.

Numbers

1 uno oono	**16** sedici saydeechee	**40** quaranta kwaranta
2 due doo-ay	**17** diciassette deechee-asettay	**50** cinquanta cheenkwanta
3 tre tray	**18** diciotto deechee-otto	**60** sessanta sessanta
4 quattro kwattro	**19** diciannove deechee-annovay	**70** settanta settanta
5 cinque cheenkway	**20** venti ventee	**80** ottanta ottanta
6 sei say	**21** ventuno vent-oono	**90** novanta novanta
7 sette settay	**22** ventidue ventee-doo-ay	**100** cento chento
8 otto otto	**23** ventitre ventee-tray	**101** cento uno chento oono
9 nove novay	**24** ventiquattro ventee-kwattro	**200** duecento doo-ay-chento
10 dieci dee-aychee	**25** venticinque ventee-cheenkway	**1,000** mille meellay
11 undici oondeechee	**26** ventisei ventee-say	**1,001** mille uno meelay oono
12 dodici dodeechee	**27** ventisette ventee-settay	**2,000** due mila doo-ay meela
13 tredici traydeechee	**28** ventotto vent-otto	**1,000,000** un milione oon meelee-onay
14 quattordici kwattordee-chee	**29** ventinove ventee-novay	**1st** primo preemo
15 Quindici kweendee-chee	**30** trenta trenta	**2nd** secondo secondo

57

The Time

In Italy the 24 hour clock is used, so times after midday are written as 1300, 1400 and so on. Another point to remember is that the Italians say, for example, "it is nine minus ten", instead of "ten minutes to nine", as we do.

Che ore sono, per favore?

Kay oray sono, pair favoray?
What time is it please?

Sono le otto.
Sono lay otto.
It is eight o'clock.

Sono le otto e un quarto.
Sono lay otto ay oon kwato.
It is quarter past eight.

Sono le nove meno un quarto.
Sono lay novay mayno oon kwato.
It is quarter to nine.

È mezzogiorno.
Ay medzojorno.
It is midday.

Sono le cinque meno cinque.
Sono lay cheenkway mayno cheenkway.
It is five to five.

Sono le sette e dieci.
Sono lay settay ay dee-aychee.
It is ten past seven.

Sono le dieci e mezzo.
Sono lay dee-aychee ay medzo.
It is half past ten.

E mezzanotte.
Ay medzanottay.
It is midnight.

la mattina
la matteena
the morning

la sera
la sayra
the evening

la notte
la nottay
the night

Time phrases

ieri ee-airee **yesterday**	quest'anno kwest 'anno **this year**	presto presto **early**	fra cinque minuti fra cheenkway meenootee **in five minutes**
oggi ojee **today**	il mese passato eel maysay passato **last month**	più presto pyoo presto **earlier**	fra un quarto d'ora fra oon kwato d'ora **in a quarter of** **an hour.**
domani domanee **tomorrow**	la settimana prossima la setteemana	fra poco fra pocko **soon**	
ieri l'altro ee-airee l'altro **the day before** **yesterday**	prosseema **next week**	più tardi pyoo tardee **later**	fra mezz'ora fra medz'ora **in half an hour**
	adesso adesso **now**	mai my **never**	
dopodomani dopodomanee **the day after** **tomorrow**			fra un ora fra oon'ora **in an hour**

Basic Grammar

Nouns

All Italian nouns are either masculine or feminine. When you learn a noun, you must learn this as well. Many nouns end with an "*o*", and these are nearly always masculine. Nouns ending with an "*a*" are usually feminine. The word for "the" is *il* before masculine (m) nouns and *la* before feminine (f) nouns.

e.g. *il libro* (the book)
la casa (the house)

If the noun is plural, the word for "the" is *i* before masculine nouns and *le* before feminine nouns.

If the word is masculine and begins with *z* or *s* plus a consonant, the word for "the" is *lo*.

If the word is masculine plural and begins with *z, s* plus a consonant, or a vowel, the word for "the" is *gli*.

If the word is singular and begins with a vowel, the word for "the" is *l'*.

Italian nouns ending in "*o*" change the "*o*" to "*i*" in the plural. Nouns ending in "*a*" usually change the "*a*" to "*e*" in the plural.

The Italian word for "*a*" or "*an*" is *un* before a masculine noun and *una* before a feminine noun.

e.g. *un libro* (a book)
una casa (a house)

Pronouns

In Italian the verb can be used on its own, without the subject pronouns. The verb endings tell you which person is referred to. Subject pronouns are only used to create emphasis.

I	*io*
you	*tu*
he	*lui*
she	*lei*
it (m)	*esso*
it (f)	*essa*
you (polite)	*Lei*
we	*noi*
you (plural)	*voi*
they	*loro*
they (m)	*essi*
they (f)	*esse*
you (plural polite)	*Loro*

Possessive adjectives

The word you use for "*my*", "*your*", "*his*" etc. depends on whether the word that follows it is masculine, feminine or plural.

You nearly always use the word for "*the*" in front of possessive adjectives.

e.g. *il nostro libro* (our book)
i nostri libri (our books)
la nostra casa (our house)
le nostre case (our houses)

	Singular		Plural	
	(**m**)	(**f**)	(**m**)	(**f**)
my	mio	mia	miei	mie
your	tuo	tua	tuoi	tue
his, her, its	suo	sua	suoi	sue
your (polite)	"	"	"	"
our	nostro	nostra	nostri	nostre
your (plural)	vostro	vostra	vostri	vostre
their	loro	loro	loro	loro
your (plural polite)	"	"	"	"

Useful verbs

Most verbs in Italian follow the same pattern as either *parlare, vendere, sentire* or *capire,* shown below. Verbs which do not follow any of these patterns are called irregular and follow different rules. *Avere* and *essere* are irregular verbs. They are used a lot because they help to form the different tenses of other verbs.

essere	**to be**
sono	I am
sei	you are
è	he, she, it is
è	you are (polite)
siamo	we are
siete	you are (plural)
sono	they are
sono	you are (polite plural)

avere	**to have**
ho	I have
hai	you have
ha	he, she, it has
ha	you have (polite)
abbiamo	we have
avete	you have
hanno	they have
hanno	you have (polite plural)

parlare	**to speak**
parlo	I speak
parli	you speak
parla	he, she, it speaks
parla	you speak (polite)
parliamo	we speak
parlate	you speak
parlano	they speak
parlano	you speak (polite plural)

vendere	**to sell**
vendo	I sell
vendi	you sell
vende	he, she, it sells
vende	you sell (polite)
vendiamo	we sell
vendete	you sell
vendono	they sell
vendono	you sell (polite plural)

sentire	**to hear**
sento	I hear
senti	you hear
sente	he, she, it hears
sente	you hear (polite)
sentiamo	we hear
sentite	you hear
sentono	they hear
sentono	you hear (polite plural)

capire	**to understand**
capisco	I understand
capisci	you understand
capisce	he, she it understands
capisce	you understand (polite)
capiamo	we understand
capite	you understand
capiscono	they understand
capiscono	you understand (polite plural)

Negatives

To make a verb negative, add *non* before the verb.

e.g. *Parlo italiano*
    I speak Italian
    Non parlo italiano
    I do not speak Italian

Questions

There are two ways you can ask a question in Italian. You can use your voice to make a statement sound like a question, or you can put the subject of the sentence after the verb.

e.g. *Capisce* You understand
    Capisce? Do you understand?
    Lei capisce? Do you understand?

Index

This index lists some words individually and some under group names, such as food. Where you will find the Italian for the indexed word, the page number is printed in italics, like this: *6*

Index of Italian words